Zen Buddhism

How Zen Buddhism Can Create A Life of Peace, Happiness and Inspiration

Sara Elliott price

Published in The USA by:

Success Life Publishing

125 Thomas Burke Dr.

Hillsborough, NC 27278

ISBN-10: 1511872713

Disclaimer

Every effort has been made to accurately represent this book and its potential. Results vary with every individual, and your results may or may not be different from those depicted. No promises, guarantees or warranties, whether stated or implied, have been made that you will produce any specific result from this book. Your efforts are individual and unique, and may vary from those shown. Your success depends on your efforts, background and motivation.

The material in this publication is provided for educational and informational purposes only and is not intended as medical advice. The information contained in this book should not be used to diagnose or treat any illness, metabolic disorder, disease or health problem. Always consult your physician or health care provider before beginning any nutrition or exercise program. Use of the programs, advice, and information contained in this book is at the sole choice and risk of the reader.

Table of Contents

Introduction

In Search of the Bull

In the pasture of the world,
I endlessly push aside the tall grasses
in search of the Ox.
Following unnamed rivers,
lost upon the interpenetrating
paths of distant mountains,
my strength failing and
my vitality exhausted,
I cannot find the Ox.

This picture and poem is first of the *Ten Bulls* pictures that describe the spiritual path followed by a Zen Buddhist monk. As you go through this book, I hope that you'll be able to relate each of the rest of the pictures and poems with you own spiritual journey.

This first poem paints a picture of confusion, depression and weakness. This is usually the point in life when a person starts seeking answers and gets into religion, philosophy, or spirituality. Zen Buddhism is one such place to look for answers. It is unique among such spiritual traditions because in Zen Buddhism you need to stop 'seeking' in order to 'find' the answers.

I'll talk about this paradoxical nature of Zen Buddhism in this book. A book on Zen Buddhism is a paradox in itself, because Zen cannot be understood through logical statements written in a book. It can only be experienced personally by practicing Zen.

So this book doesn't pretend to hold the secrets of Zen. Instead it is a collection of factual information on Zen and its practices. The book is divided into three parts; how to get started with Zen, how to practice Zen, and how to live with Zen. In this book you'll learn:

- All about Zen Buddhism and its history.

- Why it is not possible to "understand" Zen.

- The concepts used in Zen.

- How to perform Zazen or Sitting Meditation.

- Where to find a Zen Teacher to continue your learning.

- How to use art to practice Zen.

- How to apply the principles of Zen in your daily life.

All these points will only help you to practice Zen in your life but to 'get' Zen you'll have to do these practices and experience it for yourself.

The bull is a metaphor for the restless mind. This first picture, *"in search of the bull"*, represents that stage when you aren't even aware of your mind, or of the fact that your mind is the culprit behind all your problems. Zen will help you in taming this restless mind. So let's get started and try to find the bull.

Part 1: How to Get Started with Zen

Discovery of the Foot Prints

Along the riverbank under the trees,
I discover footprints.
Even under the fragrant grass,
I see his prints.
Deep in the remote mountains
they are found.
These traces can no more be hidden
than one's nose, looking
heavenward.

Chapter 1: History of Zen Buddhism

Perceiving the Bull

I hear the song of the nightingale.
The sun is warm,
the wind is mild,
willows are green
along the shore-
Here no Ox can hide!
What artist can draw
that massive head,
those majestic horns?

Sidhartha Gautama was a prince born somewhere between the 6th and 4th BCE in eastern India. At an early age he realized that acquiring wealth was not the key to alleviating human suffering. He gave up all his worldly possessions and began meditating and seeking answers to his questions through spirituality. He found enlightenment and became Gautama Buddha, whose teachings gave rise to Buddhism.

Almost a thousand years later an Indian Buddhist monk named Bodhidharma brought Buddhism to China. Here Buddhism met Taoism and Confucianism. The Sanskrit word Dhyana, which means 'to meditate', became Chan in China. Different sects of Chan Buddhism blossomed during this time, some thrived and grew while others perished or shrunk.

From China, Chan Buddhism spread farther east to places such as Vietnam, Korea, and Japan. In 1168, Myoan Eisai, a Japanese Buddhist monk went to China to study under Master Xuan Huaichang of the Linji sect of Chan Buddhism. When he came back to Japan he established the Rinzai school of Zen Buddhism. The word Zen being derived from Chan, stood for the same concept of Dhyana or meditation.

In 1217 Dogen Kigen, a young monk who had studied Rinzai Zen, felt dissatisfied by the strong focus on Koans in the Rinzai tradition and went to China to study Caodong sect of Chan Buddhism from Master Rujing. He came back to Japan to establish the Soto school of Zen, which focuses more on meditation than on Koans.

These are the two schools of Zen that are still relevant today. In short, you can say that Zen is one sect of Buddhism, but you must remember that unlike Buddhism, Zen is not a true religion. It does not have any dogmas that are usually found afflicting most religions.

In the next chapter I'll talk about how it is difficult to describe Zen using logic and reason.

Chapter 2: Understanding the Inability to "Understand" Zen

Catching the Bull

*I seize him with a
terrific struggle.
His great will and power
are inexhaustible.
He charges to the
high plateau
far above the cloud-mists,
or in an impenetrable
ravine he stands.*

Say you have to describe what honey tastes like to someone who's never tasted it before. How would you do it? If you start by saying that it's sweet, immediately the taste of sugar will come to the mind of that person. As you know the taste of honey is very unlike sugar so this person has already misunderstood what you are trying to describe. You then say that it's thick and viscous but that person can't relate to these words because he's never tasted something that's thick and viscous. You tell him it's like a thick syrup and you've confused him even more.

The more you try to describe honey in words, the more confused the person gets because the only way to understand what honey tastes like is by actually tasting it! Now, maybe someone who is extremely articulate with words can describe exactly what honey tastes like to a person who is very good at conceptualizing abstract ideas in his head. So you can say that it might still technically be possible to explain the taste of honey to someone who's never tasted it. But Zen is thousands of times more complex as a concept than the taste of honey and so it is safe to say that it is impossible to understand it through intellectualizing or philosophizing.

The ability to understand Zen becomes twice as hard when you realize that Zen actively tries to not describe itself. The whole idea of Zen is to rise above logic and reason and stop trying to use your intellect to understand the reality of the universe. In

Zen one stops seeking direct answers to one's questions and instead just tries to 'tame the bull' and become more mindful. You learn the art of being in the moment, whether it is during meditation or while performing an art form or just doing a daily chore. Instead of thinking you learn to be mindful.

By doing this what you find is not the answers to your questions but rather the dissolution of your questions. You stop being the seeker when you start living in the present moment.

To reach this state you need to practice Zen in all aspects of your life. You need to find a real Zen Teacher and learn face to face from that teacher. It is said that there has been a direct line of Zen Teachers starting all the way from Gautam Buddha who have attained the spiritual awakening by learning from their teacher. It is thought that when a teacher and student spend time together they connect on a spiritual level. When the teacher feels that the student is ready, he passes the awakened consciousness on to his student. The student becomes a Zen Teacher. In this way, Zen has been passed on from one individual to another for thousands of years.

You don't have to reach this stage in your life unless you want to become a monk and someday a Zen Teacher. Even if you just practice a few concepts of Zen, you'll clearly see its power in bringing peace to your life.

If you still don't understand the basic concept of Zen, don't worry. If you kind of get it but don't exactly know how this would work, don't worry. Try to let go of the need to understand and just go through the rest of the book and try to experience Zen by actually doing it in your life.

Before we talk about the practices that you can do to experience Zen, let's go through some common concepts of Zen.

Chapter 3: The Concepts of Zen Buddhism

Let us go through some concepts and terms used in Zen Buddhism one by one.

Zazen

Zazen is translated as sitting meditation (Za-Zen). It is the main practice in Zen and anyone can do it, even without guidance form a teacher. You just have to sit and meditate by observing your breath and in later stages observing your mind.

Koan

Koans are anecdotes or phrases that are meant to be used as an educational aid by Zen Teachers. There is no logical way of understanding these phrases and they are actually meant to break the logical thinking pattern of the student and help them "see" instead of "know". How a student reacts to the Koan can help the teacher measure the student's progress.

Mushotoku

Mushotoku is the first of the 6 states of mind or states of being that are experienced by a Zen practitioner. In this state of mind you let go of your desires. You don't seek profit in every interaction with others and you don't do every action with the ultimate aim of being successful. You simply let go of all desires for success or profit or "winning" and instead just do things for their own sake. You let go of thoughts about gain and loss and learn to just be.

This is an important phase in your development towards Satori. As you might be able to imagine, if you can learn to let go of these desires in your daily life, you'll end a lot of the suffering that you usually go through. This suffering comes from our attachment to these desires of achieving profit from every action and interaction. And when things don't happen according to our expectations, or people don't behave according to how we expected them to behave, we suffer. Mushotoku helps in ending this suffering by removing these expectations from the root. In order to start Zazen you need to stop trying to think of it as a tool to achieve spiritual enlightenment. Just do it for the sake of doing it and don't expect anything in return.

Hishiryo

Hishiryo is the state of mind that is beyond thinking and non-thinking. Like Zen, it is hard to explain in words. When you are meditating your goal is to stop all thoughts and just be aware. But this is not equal to non-thinking. Non-thinking would imply that you are blocking thoughts from arising, which is rather impossible to do. Instead, Hishiryo is the state when you are neither 'thinking' nor 'not thinking'. Thoughts arise and disappear naturally and you don't feel attached to any of them. You stop judging your thoughts as good or bad. You stop worrying about the past or future. You are simply aware of the present moment.

When you practice Zazen for a while, you can develop this state of mind and experience the natural peaceful state of mind, which is its normal state.

Zanshin

Zanshin is a state of mind that is completely aware of its surroundings and fully alert to do whatever is needed. When you are performing an art or a sport you want to be in the state of Zanshin because in this state you react instinctively to the situation in front of you. The best sportsmen in the world call it 'being in the zone'. They experience it even though they might or might not be Zen practitioners because they've spent years practicing their sport. When you reach such a state, you don't think and then act. You just act and the thinking is greatly reduced.

If a baseball batter had to consciously think about the ball before hitting it, he'd never be able to connect because everything happens so fast. By practicing for every type of ball over and over again, they develop instincts that let them understand the ball and play accordingly within a fraction of a second. If you ask such sportsmen how they did it, they won't be able to explain it because there was no conscious thinking going on. They don't know how, but they just do it. This is Zanshin.

Fudoshin

Fudoshin is a state of mind that is not bothered by negative feelings such as anger, doubt, fear, or surprise. It is the immovable mind which is confident and under complete control. When you reach this state of mind through the practice of Zazen, you become a wise person who is unshakable no matter what the situation is. You stay calm and composed and never feel fear or doubt. You have a lot of self control and don't lose your temper. You become a leader and a calm warrior in life.

Fudoshin was achieved by the Samurai who wouldn't waver from their responsibilities and stay calm even while facing certain death.

Mushin

Mushin is the state of "no-mindedness". It is the "mind of no mind". When Bruce Lee used to talk about "the path of no path" this is what he meant. It is a very high level of state of mind that can only be experienced and not described in words.

But if I were to try and describe it, I'd have to say that it is a mind that is in direct connection with the universe and is not ruled by thoughts or emotions. In this state even the ego disappears and you achieve complete clarity. It is like a clear pond that reflects the entire world around it on the surface but doesn't contain any of it within.

Satori

Satori is the highest state that a Zen practitioner can achieve. It is important to note that you can't get into Zen expecting to achieve Satori. Because if you do this, you are not in the state of Mushotoku, the first state required to practice Zen. You don't enter Zen looking for Satori but if you practice Zen you might just find it. The less you look for it, the sooner you'll find it!

Don't confuse Satori with nirvana or enlightenment. Satori is simply a return to the original most natural state of the human mind. This is the state that all life on earth, including plants and animals, are in. They are not lost in thoughts but are just one with the universe. To achieve Satori is to reach a kind of peaceful bliss that is impossible to imagine for us just like it is impossible to imagine the taste of honey for someone who's never tasted it.

Rinzai

Rinzai is one of the two important schools of Zen in Japan. It focuses mostly on using Koans to achieve insight into one's own mind. There are also further practices to attain Buddhahood after achieving Satori.

Soto

Soto is the largest school of Zen in Japan and it focuses mostly on Zazen or sitting meditation. It says that to achieve awakening, practice of Zazen is the best tool. In fact, awakening and practice of Zazen cannot be separated. It believes that if you practice Zazen, you can express the Buddhahood that is already inherent in you.

Sanbo Kyodan

Sanbo Kyodan is not a school of Zen but an organization that tries to bring Zen to the lay person. It is very popular in the west as it tries to combine the Soto and Rinzai traditions. It also tries to include other spiritual practices into a single unified practice to attain awakening.

Part 2: How to Practice Zen

Taming the Bull

The whip and rope
are necessary,
else he may stray
off down
some dusty road.
Being well trained,
he becomes naturally gentle.
Then, unfettered,
he obeys his master.

Chapter 4: Zazen or Sitting Meditation

Riding the Bull Home

Mounting the Ox, slowly
I return homeward.
The voice of my flute intones
through the evening.
Measuring with hand-beats
the pulsating harmony,
I direct the endless rhythm.
Whoever hears this melody
will join me.

Zazen is the only major practice of Zen Buddhism. It is a very simple but powerful form of meditation. You don't need to know anything about Zen to begin with Zazen. It is easy for beginners and you can start with 15 minutes and slowly increase the amount of time you spend meditating. The immediate benefits of Zazen are stress relief and clarity of mind. In the long term it can lead to the higher states of mind as mentioned in the last chapter.

What You Need

1. **A quiet place to sit and meditate.** It can be your bedroom or any other room. There shouldn't be too much noise. It should be adequately bright. It should be at a comfortable temperature according to the season.

2. **A Zafu and a Zabuton.** A Zafu is a small soft cushion traditionally used in Zazen. You can use any cushion for this purpose. A Zabuton is a mat that is placed under the cushion. Your knees will rest on the Zabuton. You can use a rug or a folded blanket for this purpose.

3. **A kitchen timer.** You can set an alarm on your phone as well. But keep the phone out of reach so that you don't get the urge to check your phone during Zazen. As a beginner, start with 15 minutes and slowly increase the time in 5 minute steps till you reach 45 minutes to 1 hour.

4. **Mushotoku.** You need this state of mind before starting Zazen. End all expectations from Zazen and just do it as a daily practice. Don't think too much about your progress or future spiritual enlightenment. Don't seek anything and don't worry about what you are getting out of this time. Even if it's a waste of time, I'm sure you can afford to waste 15 minutes of your day just sitting and doing nothing.

The Posture

It is important to sit in the correct posture to do Zazen. The correct posture will help in getting the right breathing pattern by allowing your diaphragm to move freely. The posture is also important for spiritual reasons. The posture is supposed to be rigid but relaxed, like a tiger ready for pouncing. Without the correct posture you might get drowsy and fall asleep.

Start by simply sitting cross legged on the cushion. In a simple cross legged position both your feet are under your thighs. A better position is the half lotus position in which your left leg comes up and your left foot rests on your right thigh. Your right foot remains under the left thigh. This is slightly harder to do but if you can do it comfortably you should prefer it. The best position, of course, is the full lotus position. From the half lotus you also bring your right foot up and both your feet now rest on top of your thighs. This is much harder to do and is not recommended for those suffering from knee pain or aren't flexible enough. This position is the most stable and will help in sitting perfectly still without leaning side to side or front to back.

The hands need to be in a particular position as well. The dominant hand should be placed palm up, gently resting on the thigh. The other hand will rest, also palm up, on the dominant hand so that the fingers of the dominant hand are supporting the fingers of the other hand from below. Then slightly cup both hands and bring both thumbs together. They should just barely touch each other. If you are stressed you'll notice that the thumbs are pressing into each other and you'll be reminded to relax. If you are too relaxed the thumbs will stop touching and you'll know that you need to become more alert. The thumbs should be about at the same level as your navel.

The spine should be straight and rigid but also relaxed. The neck should be straight and in line with the spine. Pull your chin back a little and try to push the air above your head with the top of your head. This will result in the right posture that is both rigid and relaxed. Keep your eyes open normally and gaze at the space about a meter in front of you. You can close your eyes if you find it hard to concentrate with open eyes but remember to not fall asleep.

The Practice

To begin Zazen simply focus on your breath. Breathe normally and don't try to force any kind of pattern. If in the beginning it remains rapid and shallow, let it be so. Slowly your breath will naturally fall to a slow and deep pattern. You need to start counting your breaths. Count the inhalation as 1 and the exhalation as 2. Continue till 10 and then restart from 1.

During this time thoughts will arise in your head, which is completely normal. Remember that your goal is not to have 'no thoughts at all'. You have no goal at all. Don't try to force a thoughtless state, as that will be completely counterproductive. Let the thoughts arise. You might even get caught in them and forget your counting. Even if you start daydreaming, it is okay. In the beginning expect this to happen often. But don't let it bother you. When you become aware that you have lost the count and are thinking about something, simply let go of the thought. Don't try to bring the thought to its logical conclusion. Just let it go and restart your count.

That is pretty much the essence of the Zazen practice. That's all you have to do! The power of Zazen comes from daily practice. The more you do it, the easier it will be to stay

focused on the counting. If you keep counting, slowly you'll realize that your breathing becomes very slow and deep. This alone has a lot of health benefits as it oxygenates the body.

Once you get good at staying focused on the count for the entire meditation period, start counting each cycle of inhalation and exhalation as one. Continue 10 cycles and then restart from 1. After doing this for a few more months you should be able to let go of the counting completely. You can begin by counting and then slowly stop counting and just be aware of your breathing. Whenever a thought pops up and you get distracted by it, restart counting and after a while stop counting again.

The idea is not to be thoughtless for the entire period but rather to be passive to the thoughts. If a thought arises but you don't lose count and it just passes naturally, then that's exactly how it should be. The problem starts when we indulge in a thought and get distracted.

To reach this stage will probably take a few years. This is all you have to do in order to explore Zen as a beginner. If you do Zazen regularly for a long time, you'll see the difference in your life first hand. Slowly you'll begin to develop the higher states of mind mentioned in the previous chapter. If you'd like to move ahead in your journey in Zen Buddhism the next step is to find an actual Zen Teacher and learn from him directly. We'll talk about this in the next chapter.

Chapter 5: Finding a Zen Teacher

The Bull Transcended

Astride the Ox,
I reach home.
I am serene.
The Ox too can rest.
The dawn has come.
In blissful repose,
within my thatched dwelling
I have abandoned
the whip and ropes.

The importance of a Zen Teacher is as complicated to understand as Zen itself. On one hand it is true that the enlightened Buddha nature is right there within us and only we can find it by practicing Zen ourselves. On the other hand there has been an unbroken line of Zen Teachers who've learned face to face from their teacher and received the Buddha consciousness directly from them.

This is also the difference between the two major sects, Rinzai and Soto, of Zen Buddhism. Rinzai Zen focuses on Koans and to understand Koans you need to have a Zen Teacher. Your teacher will tell you the Koan and gauge your understanding from your reply to the teacher. If you don't understand it correctly, the teacher will show you the flawed nature of your understanding and send you away to meditate further on that Koan.

In the Soto sect the emphasis is on Zazen. You sit and meditate and by silencing your mind you unveil the hidden Buddha nature that is already present within you. But even in the Soto tradition, Zen Teachers are present for guidance and counseling.

When to Seek a Zen Teacher

As a lay practitioner, you can achieve a lot of benefit from simply practicing Zazen. You can read books by famous Zen Masters and use your own experience to understand Zen. You can read about the different states of mind and try to achieve them on your own.

If you feel stuck in the old logical way of thinking that you've been trained to use since childhood, then you should seek a teacher. If you feel like you've achieved everything you could on your own and still want to go further into spirituality and Zen, then you should seek a teacher.

Never seek a teacher as an easy way out. A Zen Teacher cannot do the work for you. Your teacher will point you back to Zazen again and again, and you'll have to face your inner demons on your own. Don't seek a teacher just so that you can quickly 'win' the game of Zen. That's not how it works. If any "Zen Teacher" says that he can quickly teach you how to achieve happiness, peace, success, power, fame, or money, then know that that teacher is a fake and can't help you at all.

There are no crash courses in Zen. There is no quick fix formula that will help you achieve success in the material world. You can't enter Zen to find something, hoping that once you are done with it you'll move on to other things. Zen is a way of life and if you decide to enter it, you'll be committing for a lifetime. If you are ready for such a commitment then seek a Zen Teacher.

How to Find a Zen Teacher

The best place to start is your neighborhood Zen meditation centers. If you can't find a monastery or a meditation center, there must be small groups of Zen practitioners who get together to meditate and discuss Zen. You can meet likeminded people who have already been through what you are going through. You can find a Zen Teacher near you through such contacts.

Another good source for finding a Zen Teacher is the internet. Buddhanet http://buddhanet.info/wbd/ is a good place to start. It has a worldwide database of Buddhist monasteries and teachers. The AZTA (American Zen Teachers Association) http://americanzenteacher.org/ is another good source.

You might find teachers who are not affiliated to any monastery and they might be great teachers or just simple frauds. You have to be a judge of that yourself. So it is best to stick to someone who has some sort of affiliation. Zen Teachers have a strong lineage that they can trace back to hundreds of years. If your teacher refuses to tell you which lineage they belong to, then they might not be the real deal. On the other hand some frauds might falsely claim to belong to a lineage. A quick internet search, or a call to an old student can greatly clear things up for you.

Usually, most Zen Teachers or monasteries won't ask for a fee. They will accept donations but won't force you to donate. There might be one off situations when a short meditation camp or a course is being organized and they might ask for money to cover the expenses of the event. But even then it should be a modest amount.

Make sure that you find a teacher whom you can easily visit for regular sessions. There is no point in becoming a student of a famous teacher whom you can only visit once or twice a year. In the end, which teacher you find will also depend on your karma. So don't try to find the 'perfect' teacher. Go for someone who is humble and whose students feel wise and peaceful.

Part 3: How to Live with Zen

Both Bull and Self Transcended

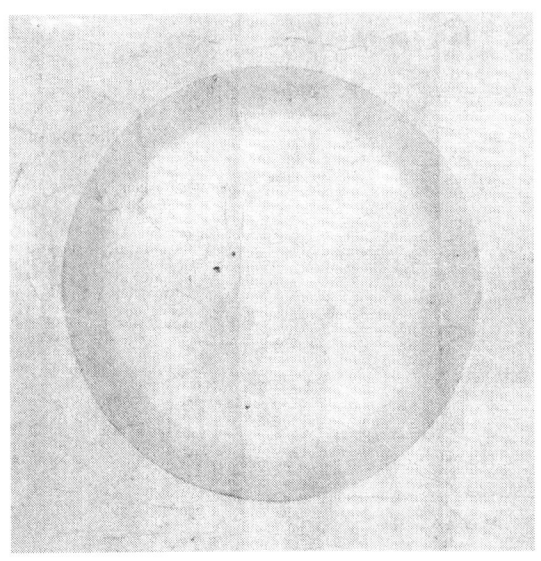

Whip, rope, person,
and Ox-
all merge in No Thing.
This heaven is so vast,
no message can stain it.
How may a snowflake exist,
in a raging fire.
Here are the footprints
of the Ancestors.

Chapter 6: Zen and the Arts

Reaching the Source

Too many steps have been taken
returning to the root
and the source.
Better to have been blind and deaf
from the beginning!
Dwelling in one's true abode,
unconcerned with and without–
the river flows tranquilly on
and the flowers are red.

Zen is closely related to several Japanese art forms. These art forms are not performed just for the sake of creating art but for the higher purpose of achieving spiritual enlightenment. To be a good artist means to have a strong connection between the mind and the body and also to have the ability to be completely present in the moment. These attributes are just as important for Zen as for art.

Chado or the Japanese tea ceremony is an art form that is entirely for the purpose of spiritual enlightenment. Other arts such as Ikebana or flower arrangement and Shodo or calligraphy, are practiced by Zen practitioners to help them attain higher spiritual levels. These art forms have the aesthetic of simplicity, moderation, imperfection, impermanence, and harmony with nature. Simplicity, moderation, and harmony with nature are values that a Zen practitioner tries to emulate in his daily life as well. Imperfection and impermanence develop non-judgment, contentment, and acceptance in the Zen monk.

Zen also has a close relation with many Japanese martial arts. Some say that the practice of martial arts is the highest practice of Zen. To understand this you have to look at martial arts as more than a sport or a personal defense technique. It requires mastery over both mind and body, and a clear connection with the present moment, in order to perform at the highest level. This outlook takes martial arts beyond a sport or even an art form and turns it into a spiritual practice.

You too can practice these art forms when you want to incorporate Zen further into your life. Even if you are not passionate about any of the Japanese Zen art forms, you can apply Zen to whatever art you are interested in. It might be painting or writing or playing a musical instrument. Every art form can benefit with a Zen attitude.

In fact, if you read biographies of famous artists, you'll find that they followed, knowingly or unknowingly, many of the principles of Zen in their art. When an artist creates a great piece of art, they are in a sort of a trance. This is a form of meditation and a way to connect to the source. This source is the source of all life and all creative expression flows from it. People have wondered for centuries about the question: 'where does creativity flow from?' Even the artists themselves aren't able to answer this question and they say things like 'it just came to me' or 'I just did it'. Note that during such creative moments there is a lack of conscious thoughts. This is because the artists have reached a meditative state where they are completely present in the moment and fully connected to the source.

You can try to achieve such states in whatever art form you want to practice. It will help your Zazen practice and your

Zazen practice will help your art. But once again I must add that don't get into Zen hoping that you'll become a great artist. As long as you want something from Zen, you will only be disappointed because it won't work with that type of a greedy mindset. It's only when you let go of all desires and expectations that you can observe the effects of Zen fully.

Chapter 7: Applying the Principles of Zen in Daily Life

Return to Society

Barefooted and naked of breast,
I mingle with the
people of the world.
My clothes are ragged
and dust laden,
and I am ever blissful.
I use no magic to extend my life;
Now, before me,
the dead trees become alive.

A daily Zazen practice is important in Zen but if you only do the meditation and then go back to "normal" mode through the rest of your day and live the same old dualistic material life then your practice becomes nothing more than a way to escape the stresses related to a materialistic way of life. To truly experience Zen and its power you have to apply its principles to your daily life.

If you follow a step-by-step process starting with simple sitting meditation on your own and then find a teacher and practice Zen through an art form, then after a while you'll naturally feel inclined to incorporate Zen into the rest of your life as well. If you can achieve this merger of Zen and the daily life you can truly experience what it means to live peacefully and harmoniously in this world. It is possible to achieve this even in a world that keeps getting more chaotic every year.

Here are a few ways to apply Zen to your daily life:

- **Turn chores into a form of meditation.** Just like an artist can meditate while making art, you can meditate while doing any mundane task such as cooking, cleaning dishes, cleaning the house etc. You can take any activity and turn it into a form of meditation. Forget about everything else and focus your attention completely on the task. Try to be completely present in the moment. Neither enjoying, nor hating the task, but simply experiencing it fully.

- **Do one task at a time.** In this superfast globalized internet world we think that multitasking is the new way to be cool, but it's just a way to build up stress. Just do one task at a time and only focus on that task. Be mindful of every task. Even if you work at a boring desk job in a boring office, focus your attention on the job at hand and forget everything else. Not only will you become better at your job but you'll also stop dreading Monday mornings! This doesn't mean you'll start loving a boring job, but you will be much more comfortable doing that job and you'll incur much less stress.

- **Do less stuff.** Once again, in this age we keep talking about productivity and being super busy to achieve success. People even sacrifice their health in order to work hard and achieve success. But if you start following Zen, you'll realize that no amount of success or money is going to bring you peace. Peace will come by actually doing less and doing it with more focus and turning it into an art form.

- **Follow a routine.** Zen monks follow a strict routine. They have a ritual for every task. It is meant to turn every task into just another opportunity to be present in the moment and practice Zen. Do the same in your life and form rituals for all your tasks. Follow a routine and be disciplined.

- **Live a simple life.** As mentioned earlier in the book, moderation is a key feature of Zen Buddhism. Apply this moderation and simplify your life. De-clutter, donate extra stuff that you don't use, downsize your house and your life. The more simply you'll live, the easier it will be to apply Zen to your life and to stay peaceful and calm. Reducing the amount of information and communication coming to you through the internet is also an important part of the simplifying process.

- **Do not use intoxicants.** Cigarettes, alcohol, drugs, happy pills, are all designed to alter the mind. Since Zen says that the true nature of the mind is the enlightened Buddha nature, you don't want to further alter it. Instead you want to remove all artificial barriers through meditation and get to that blissful core.

- **Practice compassion.** Compassion is an important part of Zen. Show compassion towards others, towards animals and plants, and most importantly, show compassion towards yourself. Do not be too judgmental and critical of yourself. Be kind to yourself and accept your flaws. Instead of beating yourself up for every mistake, just take it as another experience. Self-improvement can only happen when it comes from a place of love and contentment.

- **Take care of the body.** Zen is closely related to martial arts and there is an emphasis on having a fit and strong body. A fit mind resides in a fit body and when both mind and body are fit, it is easier to find the kind of peace that Zen talks about. To do this, exercise regularly and eat healthy and in moderation.

These are just some of the ways in which you can apply Zen to your daily life. If you do just the things mentioned in this book you'll change your life completely. But this is not even the tip of the iceberg when it comes to Zen. You can only experience it by doing it. I hope this book will help you in starting with Zen with the right mindset. The more you do it, the better you'll understand what it is about.

Conclusion

In the beginning we talked about the metaphor of the bull for the restless mind. It also represents the ego or the false self. Through out the book we saw how the bull was found, tamed and then brought to good use. This represents what you can do with Zen. It is our ego that binds us to suffering. Our restless mind causes us all the stress, anxiety, and depression. When you learn to tame the bull you get this mind under control and put it to good use. You can achieve great peace in your life by doing this.

Zen Teachers who have practiced Zen throughout their life might not have a lot of possessions or success or fame or power but they do have a lot of wisdom and peace that can make even the richest man envious. You too can achieve this by taming the bull.

But as the pictures tell us, this is not the end of the story. Eventually the bull and the individual both disappear. This represents the merging of the mind with you. After all, you and this restless mind is one and the same self. The disappearing represents the disappearance of the ego. Without an ego you simply won't feel emotions such as selfishness, greed, envy, anger, hate, lust etc. You will simply be. You will be one with everyone, every life form, and the whole universe. You will be connected to the source.

The last picture talks about the return to the society. The symbol of Zen is a full circle and so we come back to the same society that we began our journey from. But this time we've understood the illusory nature of the material world. This is a befitting and natural end to this journey because Zen is not an escape mechanism from the society. It recognizes man as part of society and it doesn't ask you to become a hermit and live all alone.

Instead, if you go through this whole journey you'll understand the true nature of the world, the society, your own ego and mind, and you'd be ready to live peacefully and harmoniously in the very same world that made you disillusioned in the first place.

Remember the 'questions' I mentioned in the beginning? Well, you might not have a direct logical answer to those questions but after reaching this stage, the questions will simply disappear. They won't exist anymore.

That's what Zen is all about. You've got to do it to experience it.

32480196R00028

Printed in Great Britain
by Amazon